A Retirement Guide
for Men

ASK CHUCK

Charles O. Jones

A RETIREMENT GUIDE FOR MEN
ASK CHUCK

iUniverse books may be ordered through booksellers or by contacting:

iUniverse
1663 Liberty Drive
Bloomington, IN 47403
www.iuniverse.com
844-349-9409

Because of the dynamic nature of the Internet, any web addresses or links contained in this book may have changed since publication and may no longer be valid. The views expressed in this work are solely those of the author and do not necessarily reflect the views of the publisher, and the publisher hereby disclaims any responsibility for them.

Any people depicted in stock imagery provided by Getty Images are models, and such images are being used for illustrative purposes only.
Certain stock imagery © Getty Images.

ISBN: 978-1-6632-4114-6 (sc)
ISBN: 978-1-6632-4113-9 (e)

Library of Congress Control Number: 2022910885

Print information available on the last page.

iUniverse rev. date: 06/14/2022

Contents

Dedication

For my brother Lou Jones: Marine Corps Veteran, Business Manager, Award Winning Poet, and Great Grandfather. Furthermore, he is relevant to the theme of this tome as the model retiree and my inspiration.

Preface

Are you retired or almost there? Perhaps just feeling old and tired? This book is for you. Why? In the first place CHUCK is beyond old at 90, yet still in reasonably good health. He walks, talks, laughs, exercises, and makes the bed. Second, he obviously cannot continue a whole lot longer, though he anxiously keeps plugging away. Third, he has stored a lot of vital information for retired guys. Those nuggets are bound to slip away as he responds to my questions.

Editors of this book manuscript pointed out that readers will puzzle over who is writing and who is playing the role of CHUCK. To clarify, they are the same person performing different functions. Charles O. writes; CHUCK remembers. Charles O. asks questions; CHUCK responds; and, magically, a brief guide to retirement is produced.

The book is organized into several broad categories of living as a retired person: At Home (how to live and work full time in your residence), Playing Outside (enjoying the outdoors without hurting yourself), Personal Matters (taking care of yourself without a formal job), and Enjoying Life (maintaining a positive attitude while declining, perhaps even dwindling, as you age). These chapters may provide you with useful lessons possibly even brighten your outlook during your "Golden Years." Whatever, I will endeavor in writing to make reading an instructional and occasionally amusing experience.

Above all learn to accommodate the changes aging brings to your life as you leave the world of employment to experience an indeterminate phase of self -definition. Done right you may live to be 90 and beyond. Keep your chin up and your stride lengthy.

Chapter One

At Home

"It takes a heap of living to make a house a home." (Edgar Guest). CHUCK and his friend, Pat Patterson re-cast this saying to: "It takes a heap a heapa to make a heap a home." Both work here. Having personally done so often—that is, living a house into a home—CHUCK'S first and most vital recommendation for a newly minted retiree is simply *"Stay home."* Travel? Of course. But hey man, with all this freedom consider the basics defining you—tools, work clothes, books, adult beverages, boots, golf clubs, bowling ball, fishing gear, football-watching chair with accompanying drink rest—you know, ordinary guy stuff.

Furthermore you know where the stuff is, each item having found a designated spot over the years. Starting over? Yikes. In retirement you're too old to look for a fresh nest, especially a place run by much younger "specialists" trained to program the rest of your life, trading those activities you truly like for those people referred to as "staff" imagine you should like. Nix on the retirement condo or bungalow, designed by commercial-oriented whizzes.

Having settled the basic issue of location, let's explore parts of your home with which you may not be familiar.

For example, you may not be well acquainted with the kitchen in your own home. If so, as CHUCK was not, this vital room offers opportunities for guys with time on their hands. But your work there often requires sensitivity to who ordinarily rules that realm. Perhaps you have already formed a partnership, maybe cooking together or trading off you for me or vice versa. If so, congratulations. Otherwise, like CHUCK, you are assigned related tasks: table setting and clearing, washing pots and pans, possibly loading and unloading the dishwasher (careful—more to it than it seems), and waiter duties for guests. These tasks are not noble work but necessary and helpful if you stay out of the way. Oh, and take note: Just as your stuff has found its place, so, too, has the Chef's paraphernalia, not to be misplaced. "Where did you put my spatula?" Note the word "my" in the question, which designates possession.

An equally fundamental opportunity is your fitting into cleaning routines. Let's back up to the overruling principle in home management: Keep it clean. How can you help? Start by identifying the regions you occupy most. Claim those spots as your responsibilities. Learn how to use the available equipment, notably vacuum cleaners, mops, dusting and wash rags, window cleaners, spot and stain removers. CHUCK prefers a damp rag for dusting. No chemicals there. Just dip the rag in water, wipe gently, and wring it out so the dirt is displayed in the sink. Rinse it out often. Works very well. This freshening up can be prideful work in making your home comfortable and, don't discount this point, the place will smell good. Cleanliness has a welcoming aroma, especially if your rag contains a drop or two of PineSol or a similar cleansing product.

The cleaning routines also lead one into another part of the home with which you may be unfamiliar: the laundry room. Containing machinery vital to living the good life, this room should be of interest to men. Your significant other likely knows how to run the washer/dryer and can therefore tutor your way into managing these units. The manufacturers keep changing how the machines work—presumably toward greater efficiency and effectiveness but with many dials and buttons. However, when the clothes, sheets, towels, etc., are clean and dry they have to be sorted, folded, and stored— again necessary but hardly glamourous work. You can do it, however, with some personal satisfaction if not contributing to bragging rights with your golf or fishing buddies.

You need an office. Let's call it that. Some folks refer to a "man cave." That's okay, though CHUCK doesn't like the term—unnecessarily contrived. The point is, you need some place in your home to call yours. It can hold the stuff that defines you. In CHUCK'S case this room is full of shelves filled with books and photos revealing his interests, indeed his profession as an academic. He could easily get rid of most of the books, having read them some years back and seldom pulling them down now. But, hold on, emptying the shelves would be like laying him away. Not yet. Goodness, CHUCK even wrote a few and he likes seeing them filling out one of the shelves. Furthermore, decades ago a dear friend taught him to use an author's book as a file cabinet for his or her correspondence. Thus, many titles are stuffed with personal memories.

Other CHUCK stuff is in the study. For example, a computer and printer, three desks, a file cabinet, presidential campaign buttons, old photos of politicians, comfortable reading chairs, and four storage closets chockful of files, more books, old computers, and God knows what else.

One bookshelf section is reserved for a collection of single malt scotches, with proper sipping glasses and several books on those elegant brews. CHUCK came to appreciate single malts in the late 1990s during a year in England. Tom Tinsley, a virologist at Oxford University, was his tutor. He learned how and when to drink single malts and how they vary. Soon he had several brands, occasionally had tastings with friends. His favorite over time has been Laphroag. Very peaty. Hold it in your mouth, move it about before swallowing for a complete tasting. Fantastic sensations. Repeat that exercise with every malt sampling. Oh and sip modest amounts. No ice—malts are very different from blended scotches. "On the rocks" is not recommended.

Alas, presently CHUCK seldom imbibes but likes seeing the handsome bottles there in in the study as delightful memories. Ah the ravages of aging. Reading an English or Scottish murder mystery on a cold winter evening is sure to lead to pulling the cork, pouring a finger or two, adding a few drops of pure water. Do create this kind of memory shelf of your own. Single malts do not self -drain. They rest easy, awaiting inheritance by some fortunate lad or lassie.

A counterpart room for many guys is a workshop. Tools, tools, and more tools. Marvelous workshop odors from wood, sawdust, paint, oils, stains, used work aprons, projects near completion. Do keep the shop well ventilated! CHUCK has scads of tools but no workshop as such (see "garage" below). Guys with serious workshops basically have no problems retiring. They can move easily from the office to their shop with a chance for creative, satisfying work. Do consider including a radio for talk or music as background. No TV— too distracting and frequently dumb. Perhaps also include a small apartment-type fridge for housing a few brewskis.

All of which leads us to the GARAGE. This is your domain, fella. If you don't have one, start building. Provide ample room for "stuff." Include lots of shelf space, industrial-size hooks, perhaps a corner for a workshop table with a large peg board, and definitely a mud room as entry into the house from the garage. Outfit this entry space to hang jackets, store boots, shelve work gloves and caps, store the dog's "stuff" in its place. You will also have to estimate the full range of gardening equipment, plus sprays, fertilizer, seeds, and the like. Whatever amount of space you plan for these spaces, double it.

Understand that the garage fills up rather quickly with what you don't know where to put presently. And at least once a year the garage must be cleaned and rearranged. CHUCK personally hates the job. Yet one is stimulated to press on only because you know, in the end, the space becomes functional again with cleaning and sorting. Do not allow the accumulation to alter the principal purpose of the space—housing your vehicles. I have often seen garages leaving no room for the cars. That is not a pretty sight. Among other bad effects: you begin to lose track of stuff when the space is overstored and the cars will fare poorly outside. After all their protection was the garage idea at the start.

Do be creative in what goes into your garage. CHUCK likes tools and has collected them through the decades, mostly at flea markets. He prefers old tools (pre-digital); hand-made; out-of-the-ordinary (often doesn't know what they are); artistic, even sculptural; and those tools that can be displayed interestingly throughout the house as well (pending approval of your spouse). Refinishing some tools is very satisfying, particularly wood planes, tool handles, and bigger pieces: e.g., harness, vices, potato and seed planters, a vinegar pump, railroad car wedge (gorgeous), wooden boxes filled with tools, conversation pieces all. Boring? No way. CHUCK re-discovers an antique tool ever so often, cleans and polishes it and displays it in a choice spot in the house, often by the fireplace. Appealing? The ultimate.

Other of CHUCK'S collections merit some show time as well. Among the rarest sets are license plates from the state of South Dakota. If you have a map handy, CHUCK was born in Worthing, raised in Canton. I kid you not. Listen to this and promise not to be envious. His plates are not for sale in spite of their obvious big bucks value. His oldest South Dakota plate is dated 1942, with three others in the 1940s. The collection is in sequence in the 50s, as are seven of 10 in the 60s. The state added Mount Rushmore on the plate in 1953. And, here we are surely talking serious money. CHUCK has two trailer plates from 1954 and 1956! Total South Dakota plates: 25. P.S.: Also in the collection are plates from other states in which he has lived: Arizona, Pennsylvania, Virginia, and Wisconsin—some in sequence. The reader can, unquestionably, sense the pride shown with this collection and may well be stimulated to match it. CHUCK concedes there are innumerable auto plate collections across the country— many, likely most, considerably more varied and complex than his set. But, hey, permit him a little home state pride.

To urge you further CHUCK offers other displayable collectables.

Presidential campaign buttons by the hundreds. Earliest: 1896. They are displayed primarily in the study. Largest? LBJ in 1964. Oddest item? "Win with Willkie" handkerchief in 1940. Hmmm? What do you do with a hanky? "You Can't Lick Our Dick!" Nixon in 1972. Most definite? "No Third Term" in 1940, directed against FDR. Also displayed in the study are presidential inaugural medals, much less interesting but nicely presented. CHUCK'S friend, Robbert Jones (no relation and his first name is spelled correctly), has nearly a complete collection of these medals. Impressive. Three of his grand-children, Cooper, Henry, and Emily, have shown great interest in these collections, yet another reason for holding on to "stuff."

Beer and Ale Bottles. CHUCK had some over 200 such bottles displayed on a top shelf in the garage. It was a beautiful sight—all different, a third were English and Scottish. "Uff-da," "OldHooky," and "Old Fart" were honored favorites. Guys loved it, spotting those brands having given them real pleasure. Alas the collection was dumped a few years ago. Really. Perhaps the dumbest move in an otherwise half-smart life.

Maps. Now we are getting serious. Guys CHUCK'S age still use a M.A.P., not a G.P.S. when traveling (truth is the GPS is mighty handy, maps, however, more nostalgic and truly provide the lay of the land). These old guys keep several maps in their cars, including road atlases (now mostly accompanied by a magnifying glass). The large collection back in the house is organized by region, states, and cities (foreign and domestic). Every so often they are reviewed and reorganized. A while back, many domestic state and city maps were available from "filling" stations. Dozens in CHUCK'S collection were issued before interstate highways were built.

Playing with one's maps can be great fun and highly absorbing. For example, the resident map of West Berlin preceded the takedown of the Berlin Wall, which is depicted on the map. One all-time favorite is a walking map along the Thames River between villages, Oxford to Reading. Fabulous. CHUCK and his wife have walked most of those pathways.

<u>CAPS</u>. While not associated directly with the garage, billed caps surely belong in CHUCK'S collections. His dozens of these head ware were bound to proliferate as associated with expanding baldness, along with what to give the old man by children, grandchildren, other family members, and friends (socks being the alternative).

So the number of caps was bound to grow, sustained as well by Grandpa's willingness to wear the protective covering they offered. Naturally enough those worn most are fewer than ten. Of those at least two or three were University of Wisconsin Badger caps (of the total of 12 UW toppers). Other favorites are the Pittsburgh Pirates and Steelers (two, son Dan), Wintergreen Resort (the dog), U.S. Army Retired

(Granddaughter Annabel), The Brookings Institution, and Political Science (Pat Patterson).

The U.S. Army Retired cap has a special story. CHUCK'S brother, Lou was wearing his Marine Corps cap during a vacation on a North Carolina Beach. Likewise CHUCK was wearing his Army cap. Having lunch with wives, they called for the check. The waitress said the tab had been paid, pointing to a man sitting at a nearby table with his daughter. Looking to us, he said: "Thank you for your service." We were stunned, thanking him profusely. Subsequently, CHUCK often has worn his Army cap when going out to lunch. Alas, for me, the North Carolina beach experience was a "one off." Lou, however, scored with a drink wearing his Marine Corps cap at lunch elsewhere,

Back to Rooms. What have I left out of the home? Actually a room you may have put at the top of the list. I have saved that spot for last given its more private utility. You no doubt guessed correctly: The bathroom. You will be spending more time in this location as the years pass. Trust me on this one. More and more this room will develop into Health Central. Given its major body support functions, try either for a personal room or some exclusivity—e.g., time assigned to you in a joint bathroom. As with the garage, you may want to build one to suit your increased variety of functional needs.

Crucial to the effective use of this room is sufficient space for the growing body of paraphernalia: pills, creams, powders, lotions, potions, and schedules. You will be making and living with changes, for example, losing hair where you hoped to keep it; having it pop up where it is annoying—in your ears and nose. Organization is essential, as is timing. You need to keep so much in order. A pad and pencil will help. Pay attention to sequences. Try to stay ahead of growths. Keep looking your best, no simple task with each passing year. Don't forget body odor when going out in public, but don't overdo the sweet lotions as they can overwhelm a cocktail hour and suggest you are hiding something, which you probably are.

Bathroom body functions can leave unpleasant aromas. Old-fashioned remedies work well for neutralizing odors. For example, striking and snuffing out matches is effective, typically requiring a minimum of two strikes. Do try not to set something on fire as you may not be nimble enough to extinguish the flame. Sprays are useful, depending on the chemical interactions. CHUCK'S father-in-law favored keeping the window open, hoping for a breeze. This technique was revealed on a ski vacation in Arosa, Switzerland, where breezes were brisk and cold. Result? Completing one's activity was bracing, to say the least. But the room was fresh.

The thing is what is happening as you age may make your eliminations more odiferous. So don't give up on the issue. Keep on it, making life as bright and fresh as possible in your declining years. At CHUCK'S age, he has had a lot of direct experience on this matter.

Finally, the bathroom traditionally houses the implements for cleansing your body. How and when you perform these functions is, of course, subject to personal preferences. The best CHUCK can offer are experience-based hints. Shower or tub bath? On the Seinfeld television series, Cosmos Kramer pointed out that a hot bath was trying to clean sitting in your own filth. A decent enough observation. However, old guys typically have aches and pains. They can manage by taking potentially damaging pain pills. Or slip into a hot bath for a relieving soak. That practice relaxes your tired, old body for pain free slumber and pleasant dreams. Not guaranteed, of course, but worth a try.

Scrubbing those digits? Absolutely. Many times a day and especially after touching various things. Nuff said. Hair and head management? If you have hair to manage lucky you. Preserve it; move it around, if necessary. If you don't have it, or, like CHUCK, just on the edges, keep the noggin as clean and clear as possible. Other unsightly substances try to grow on these open fields—lumps, pimples, dark spots, and scabs. Make the face as free, shiny, and kissable as possible. Check out the limitless number of creams and potions designed to help out.

Mouth? Scrub the teeth you have left. Trade off using a tooth brush with sloshing a mouth wash. Oh, and spit into the toilet not the sink so as to avoid drainage issues. What comes up with plunging is not pretty, often black and slimy, thus requiring removal of the slick and yukky residue. Best of luck in finding a place to dispose of it.

Easing into retirement? CHUCK had a glorious first year. Invited to Nuffield College, Oxford University 1998-99, he lectured, managed graduate seminars, and worked on research and writing. All activities were genuinely pleasant. Often academics can "retire" into a sizable portion of their normal workload of research. That was surely CHUCK'S first year, postponing the more tedious aspects of retirement in a grand and related setting.

Enough already. CHUCK has you mostly clean, smelling on the plus side of pleasant, exuding confidence in how you are living a purposeful and presentable life in retirement—thus ready to interact with your new world. We turn next to outdoor activities which may contribute positively to your job free aging experience.

Chapter Two

Playing Outside

Step outside your home, pad of paper in hand or a hand-held recording device. You have very likely spent a lot of time providing an attractive landscape for your home or, perhaps, spent a lot of money to have someone else plan and landscape the property. Now you have the time and opportunity to make improvements and undertake projects postponed by a busy work schedule. Let your mind lead you to new efforts. Presently in his twenty-fifth year of retirement, CHUCK can assure you few activities are more exhilarating than shaping and reshaping the land on which your home rests. However large or small this property is yours. Mark it as such, personalize it. If others like what you do, so much the better. Your effort will be a fine topic of conversation. But mostly suit yourself. Let each project satisfy YOU, coaxing you outdoors from watching TV, reading a newspaper, drinking your third cup of coffee, or staring at the wall.

Great. Now work yourself around the property. Write down whatever occurs to you, don't hold back any proposal or erase one prematurely. Let them all rest on the pad to be evaluated later, even then preserve these thoughts as they may link up with other new ideas. Oh, and as a personal favor to

CHUCK, consider paths and/or trails. To do so will please him and even considering these walkways will enliven you. Guidance for making pathways will follow.

Take your time on this exercise. Savor each listing, imagining how it will enhance the property and reward you. Once back inside review every entry, making notes on what equipment and which materials will be required, as well as the phases of the work, length of time for completion, and assistance needed. Can you manage it alone? Ranking the entries is useful for deciding where and when to start, as well as how the projects relate, one with the others. For example, in the process of designing pathways, CHUCK realized he was revealing rock outcroppings. These natural formations came to be priorities that did not make his original list, projects well suited to the choice and development of the pathways. This discovery was very instructive and immensely satisfying.

A number of examples from various home locations will be introduced. The purpose is to describe a wide selection of projects, seeking to illustrate purpose and reasoning. The examples are not offered as ventures for the readers. Obviously, we don't know the size and features of readers' surroundings. Rather the cases offered are meant to stimulate thinking of what suits your interests and spread. Above all, the goal is to confirm the excitement and personal rewards associated with working outside. Maybe the individual cases will lead to copying some aspects of CHUCK'S efforts. If so, let him know.

<u>Get Acquainted with Your Tools</u>. On your way outside, stop by the garage to review your tool inventory. As the saying goes: "Nothing happens without tools." You likely have a standard set for gardening: rakes, shovels, hoe, garden bow saw, mower, clippers (several sizes), and knee pads. Here are a few additional items CHUCK recommends: hand and swing scythes, a four-pronged rake (deep prongs), limb saw, ax or adz, rock moving bar, sledge hammer, blower, heavy electric cords, pole saw, pick, a rock hammer (double head), and a beer opener at the ready with the completion of a work period. Drinking the golden brew not recommended on the job itself.

In this second group, CHUCK is virtually immobile without the four-pronger and the double-head rock hammer. Both are essential for building a rock garden and lining a path. The four-pronger is a rake with muscles. Its prongs are longer than a standard rake, thus able to dig deeper in managing the soil and dislodging buried rock (warning: also buried cables).

The rock hammer is sort of like a hand-held adz with a hammer on one side, flat pick on the other. The tool serves well for hands and knees digging and pulling rock from the soil. Equally useful are double pick hand-held instruments. These two tools in CHUCK'S collection were given to him by a colleague's wife at the University of Pittsburgh. Her father was a brick layer, a noble vocation. Check any Winston Churchill biography. Knowing of CHUCK'S interest in tools the "gifter," (Eleanor by name) judged correctly he would use these tools. He has done so in her honor. Bless her—one remembers such thoughtful gifts forever.

Often the best place to purchase your tools is a flea market, a second-hand or antique store. Virtually all of CHUCK'S collection came from these sources. Garden tools typically do not wear out, or even get tired. Moreover used tools have smooth handles, do not need to be broken in, are much easier to use, and less likely to result in slivers. Think ahead to the projects and evaluate your existing tool inventory in determining what is lacking, as well as estimating how one tool (for example, a four pronger) will serve multiple purposes.

Good. Let's review some outdoor projects.

Bird Baths. Consider something simple yet necessary. You can't have too many bird baths. As brother Lou observes about many things: "Placement is everything." So check out your garden and yard for convenient spots likely to be attractive to dirty birds. Those places should be shady. Birds don't need hot water for a bath. Their tubs should vary in depth. Look for natural rock depressions. Birds seem to prefer them. Welcome other thirsty animals—dogs, frogs, chip monks, and squirrels. Keep the vessel filled with fresh water. It is bothersome for birds to settle on a comfortable bath only to find it cold-stone empty or filled with debris. Brush clean the bowl before filling. I'll never forget being asked by a young girl what I was doing while brushing a natural bath location. I explained and she exclaimed: "Oh, I didn't know you had to clean a bird bath." Well, dah!

There are few more satisfying sights than a bird doing a full-scale wash down, under-the-wings, splashing in a bath surrounded by flowers and rocks. Nearby a bench is occupied by you having your morning coffee. Now that's retirement at its peak. Carry that scene in mind as you work around your present garden or gardens. If you already have placed a bench or two in the garden, let that influence where you place the new bird bath.

On a related note, you may also favor bird houses. Many folks have been successful in such ventures, either making or buying them. Bluebird houses seem to be popular. Sorry we can't help you there. CHUCK has had no luck getting birds to live in his bird digs. Maybe it's the placement. Brother Lou is good at it, as he is on most outdoor work.

On the other hand, birds have settled into spots never designed for their residence and chick birth. One such was a natural wood sconce tacked to the front porch wall. It was designed for holding dried flowers. A mama bird settled in when the sconce was empty. She built a nest, had babies, and moved out, repeating the same exercise the following year and subsequently. Great pleasure to watch over time and into fledging.

On one occasion mama bird pestered us until we removed the flowers in place and she then took over once we emptied her dwelling. Along the way she had tried nesting in the garage and the back decks, even flying in the dining room at one point, obviously thinking: "Jesus, don't these people catch on?"

I do need to clarify how little CHUCK knows about birds, save for what he has read and forgotten from guide books. That condition likely places him in the majority of old guys. He has, however, enjoyed bird presences around the home and has over the years endeavored to provide means for them to keep clean.

I should record, however, that CHUCK'S eldest son, Joe B, has a friend, Letitia, who is a bona fide ornithologist. She often practices her craft as a Ranger for the National Park Service during the summer. This woman knows a lot about birds, frequently traveling world-wide on birding excursions. Joe B has developed into a talented photographer of the species.

<u>Pathmaking</u>. CHUCK does know about paths and trails. Indeed, he is an experienced designer of such byways, in truth, a legitimate "pathologist," one of a largely unorganized but enthusiastic mass of guys. Paths by their very nature are dynamic, even vibrant. Their creations virtually speak, asking you to follow along. "Walk me, please. Enjoy what I offer. Oh, and what is offered will differ with each stroll—same

path, different stroll. We, the paths of America, guarantee rewards." Pathologists like to think of their routes as living mediums. Sometimes while reading or doing a crossword puzzle, CHUCK'S mind follows a favorite path through the woods and bridging a stream, dog alongside, each absorbing the path's offerings anew.

How about this anecdote for a satisfying moment? Recently, a neighboring eleven-year old gal with the appealing name of Ellie, a lover of pathways, told CHUCK she made a map of his paths! Life doesn't provide rewards any better than that. Alas, CHUCK failed to ask her for the map so he could make a copy. Lesson: keep notes, save maps, take photos.

How one makes a path depends heavily on its setting. Thus, if the location is within a garden, the path likely is for purposes related to what is there. Strolling through flowers, harvesting vegetables, trimming growth, transplanting, watering, fertilizing—all such activities are facilitated by paths.

Placing a bench along the way is also a bonus so as to observe and profit from your work, as well as a spot to place tools and watering cans. While thinking about tools, do tag them, perhaps with colored ribbons. They are easily misplaced given their typical earthy shades. Leaving them in the middle of the path rather than alongside in the leaves is also a good idea. CHUCK'S maxim: "A misplaced tool is a lost tool until you buy a new one." Voila! "There it is, now I have two."

Staying with the garden path, best to introduce a universal issue—that of path lining. CHUCK is a proponent, save for lengthy paths. Once again consider the setting. Is material available right there in the yard or acreage? Etching can be achieved with rocks, bricks, limbs, brush, or gravel. CHUCK recommends small to medium sized rocks or bricks for a garden. They look neat and can be stomped or hammered to hold their place. Also consider lining the whole garden with large rocks to delineate it from the lawn. You may even want to fence in the garden, thus making a naturally cozy nest combining work and relaxation. Include a bench and at least one bird bath. I like picturing you there right now.

Time now to be going somewhere, the very purpose of a path. CHUCK has made paths with destinations in western Pennsylvania, southwestern Wisconsin, and central Virginia. In these locations acreage was added to the original home site precisely for the purpose of "pathing." In Indiana Township, Allegheny County, Pennsylvania, over five acres was added to the four where the home was located. A stunning piece of land begged to be worked into a living space. Paths were fashioned through the trees, down to a stream, and over small ditch-like depressions.

With a local power company's permission CHUCK and their two sons felled an unused electric line pole, sawed it in half, and built a bridge over one deep depression with a stream below. With planking, it was a prideful construct in the woods. All paths led to a point where two streams joined. The Jones boys cleared underbrush to delineate the paths but did not line them given their length. All guests were trotted out to the bridge and down to the stream crossings. "Well, you have to" was a proper explanation.

The Wisconsin paths varied. Those near the home in Cross Plains, Dane County, worked their way through a neighboring lot we purchased leading to a point facing west over Route 14 near a glacial pond. The path then dropped down to the pond and along a forest road working back to the home and further to the main road through the neighborhood. It was a delightful walk through woods in all seasons. Best time? During a light snowfall in winter. As indicated, sizable portions of the walk were provided by a primitive road used much earlier in the development of the neighborhood. Connecting paths were formed primarily by removing brush. Frequent use aided in preventing the regrowth of vegetation. Occasionally the paths were used for cross-country skiing. And these paths were graced by first Jones standard poodle—Bonnie. She was a perfect fit. You can't have paths without a dog and you can't have a dog without paths. Compatible partners.

The second pathway set in Wisconsin was near Spring Green in Iowa County. Dale Pforr, a realtor in Spring Green served in purchasing the house in Cross Plains. He tempted CHUCK and Vera to consider purchasing land in Iowa

County, noting that prices were presently low. One chunk of land in particular was notably attractive: a 90-acre farm with a barn, attached milk house, and a collapsed log structure once serving as a farm house. The property was fenced and had a running stream through the acreage, Snead Creek.

Dale drove in, passing by the barn and up a dirt road to a field of blooming golden rod waving in the breezes. It was breathtaking. The Joneses bought it—a farm of their own! Truth to tell, not much farming was possible on the property. It served better as a county park with bluffs, a stream, cliffs, small fields, rock outcroppings, wildflowers, and some existing trails. The property was a rich assortment of destinations, a pathologist's dream.

CHUCK began making paths with a sizable but barely functioning lawn mower. He soon realized this tired machine would not do the job. Off to Farm and Fleet in nearby Dodgeville in search of a walking mower with bicycle wheels, sort of an industrial-sized mechanism prepared to cut some serious tall grasses along the creek, on the bluffs, across the fields, and alongside the ridges. As expected, Farm and Fleet had exactly what he was looking for, bought it, brought it to the farm, tested it and stored it in the milk house. The mower worked perfectly. CHUCK set about "path-a-sizing" the farm for sensible hiking, cross-country skiing, berry picking, and picnicking. On weekends, the family could hardly wait to drive to the farm. Bonnie was a regular pal on each trip.

The reader may carry this image in the mind: CHUCK managing the mower, path slowly revealing itself, Bonnie plodding along behind with the Poodle's version of a quizzical look. Most often the two would work toward a bench on a high point for lunch and treats for Bonnie. From that point one could look back with pride on a newly-created path. CHUCK believed it was Heaven on earth, well at least in Iowa County.

Path making was but one of the retirement activities on the farm. The red barn badly needed repair. Several holes in the roof permitted rain to pour onto the barn floor with unfortunate results. Large doors at either end required stabilizing as they hung loosely on tracks. The log cabin had fallen in on itself. Several logs were salvageable for use back in the gardens near the Cross Plains home. And Snead Creek needed a walking bridge across, also requiring support from the cabin logs. A collapsed horse barn required a full-scale clean up job. In short, a great deal of work was needed, frankly to CHUCK'S delight. A local farm building reconstruction firm was hired for the roof, flooring, and barn door repairs. The rest was managed by CHUCK, Vera, and Bonnie—both sons then off to teach skiing and summer jobs. Overall, the work produced a magnificent result, a sheer pleasure to visit, hike, picnic, smell the air, and express pride of ownership. One other note: A resident hunter and his son were allowed to hunt on the property. Their contribution? Occasional monitoring to prevent unwelcome hunters use of the acreage.

Now for Central Virginia: Additional acreage for path making was not necessary for the first Virginia home just outside Charlottesville in Albemarle County. The new property contained some over 10 acres. In leaving Pittsburgh for Charlottesville CHUCK and Vera were moving from a four-person to a two-person live together family, both sons then in college. The property dropped down to a running creek on its way to a large reservoir. Ah, woods, rock outcroppings, and destinations. Additionally there was a fenced-in field with a neighbor's in-resident cattle. Paths to Ivy Creek already existed. More were added, including one leading to a point overlooking Ivy Creek. Another led directly to where a canoe was kept near the creek.

One regret. Two old buildings were on the property. The original home was reportedly built in 1805. A cabin was added in the 1840s. There were at least two areas with evidence of having been used to discard junk—bottles, cans, pots, etc. CHUCK intended to do some exploring in these spots, perhaps later with the aid of his archaeologist son. Didn't happen. CHUCK and Vera moved before exploring the potential goldmine of treasures, what some misguided folks call "trash." Take notice, reader. Follow through immediately with new sites, at least to verify their potential.

No regrets, however, for a very large garden had existed behind the home. Vera managed this farm-like property planting corn, asparagus, pumpkins, tomatoes, beans, lettuce, peppers, and much more. The 50'x50' area had been a pig yard at one point so the soil was a rich black plot instead of Virginia red clay. Fresh, out of the garden lunches were very special for trail makers.

With the move from Pittsburgh to Virginia, CHUCK and Vera bought a ski cottage at Wintergreen Resort in the Blue Ridge Mountains. A path was bound to show up. Sure enough. There was a classy fantasy castle-like rock formation on the property to the rear of the cabin, extending over to a trail working its way down to a rock precipice overlooking the valley. The descending trail was called "The Plunge." Creating a trail to these two rock formations virtually happened on its own. These pathways got used regularly by all four generations—great grandparents, grandparents, parents, and grand kids. Wintergreen itself is a large network of trails through trees, over rocks, by cliffs and rock outcroppings, and to countless destinations.

CHUCK can, to this day, hear Annabel, Joe B's then three-year old daughter, saying as he stumbled: "That's okay, Chuck. It's not rocky here." He moved over to her on the path and took her outstretched hand.[Note: Fact is, rocks— small, large, and huge—are everywhere in the Blue Ridge

Mountains. If not on the surface, dig a few inches and they will appear joyfully marking their freedom.]

Then there was the creation of "Jones Park" in Virginia. In 2015 an adjacent lot to the new Wintergreen home was purchased. It was a virgin piece of land. CHUCK was ecstatic. Trees, brush, rocks, rock outcroppings, mounds, levels, groves, natural stone walls, limbs and fallen trees—truly work projects for decades to fashion a park. Several rocks were huge. Most prominent was a rock and stone-based mound overlooking existing rock gardens on the original property. Magnificent! This rock had been coveted for years. Now owned, it was ready for pathological treatment, eventually with benches added.

CHUCK, then in his 18ᵗʰ year of retirement at the purchase of the new lot, could not wait to start working on the property. In examining the grounds, it became clear forest growth covered most of the rock outcroppings. The home was on a lot of similar proportions and it was apparent from what had been uncovered on the home lot that similar treasures would be hidden next door. So to work. At the time, CHUCK as a retiree was completing his memoirs and a second edition of a "very short introduction" to the American presidency. These projects had to be put on hold, at least until completing a survey, resulting in a rough mapping of points to be revealed. Identifying such locations aided in marking the design for paths from one outcropping to the next.

Presently, 2022, CHUCK has completed pathways on three quarters of the lot. Several rock outcroppings have been uncovered, several paths have joined those on the original lot, benches have been added along with small rock displays, and an engraved rock placed off the street at the entry to the lot reading: "Donna's Path." A neighbor died of cancer in 2018. She was among the first to walk the paths created at the time. The stone memorializes her, as do woodland sunflowers planted along the edge of the property.

In the Spring and Summer of 2020 the "south 40" was worked on. A path was cleared over bed rock, ferns were transplanted in one clear section, a brush wall (see below) was extended to the National Park boundary where the brush wall carries along north on the border. Much work remains on this piece, fortunately. Etching the boulders is a prime task as it frames their beauty and gives them "destination" status. Two trees along the border carry National Park Service (NPS) notices. CHUCK likes those posts.

Among the most striking rock outcroppings on the new lot is a section along the southern border. It contains impressive boulders leading up to a solid stone wall and beyond to the street. At this spot the ashes of Othello were spread. This remarkable cat was a close friend of three Jones dogs. Othello died in his late teens. For a tribute, a stone marker was placed reading: "Othello's Grotto." See the book cover. Be certain to visit the memorial stone should you come by.

<u>Making a Path</u>. The pathway descriptions illustrate the many variations of their formation. Mowing tall grasses in the case of the Wisconsin farm; removing brush, re-locating rock, and joining abandoned roads at the Cross Plains home; following streams in the Pittsburgh environs; and working toward Ivy Creek in Albemarle County, Virginia. The adjacent lot to the present Wintergreen home demanded the most planning and finagling. It was the most natural, lacking development—sort of an untouched half acre of the Blue Ridge Mountains. Accordingly it offered challenges and provides lessons in forming pathways.

A first lesson in the planning phase stands out from observing a dramatic feature of the lot CHUCK and Vera now live on. Rocks dominate the landscape and, as with people, no two are alike. Some are huge, some just big and flat, others seem small but are only peeking out, many are inviting use for bordering the paths. When working on a rock garden in front of the home, one was amused by this question from passersby: "Where did you get the rocks?" CHUCK'S response: "Take a look at the surroundings." The Blue Ridge Mountains are the Rocky Mountains of the east.

The purpose of an initial walk around a rock-dominant acreage is to identify some bare stretches or sections where you can spot interesting rock outcroppings once forest growth is removed. Next is the process of clearing the ground, which, in addition to grassy or weedy cover will likely include surface rocks usable as border. This work is mostly a hands-and-knees endeavor and may well involve a second or third study. Why? Because rocks move and you have made spaces into which they may re-settle. Many large relatively flat rocks can be incorporated into the path. In fact, they often are too large and well established to budge—inviting back strain for the overly-ambitious and insensitively optimistic pathologist.

Okay, now you are making progress (notice how I imagine you are incorporated into the text). Walk the completed sections and push ahead. You are likely to find that piling bordering rocks along the way eases the tasks of lining once you are satisfied the path is progressing as you intended. You may also consider lining the path with downed limbs, using a clipper or limb saw to fashion a straight and clean lining. These border limbs may either serve permanently or temporarily pending sufficient rock availability. CHUCK uses both, promising himself later to replace limbs with rock.

A practical test of developing paths is to bring along your dog. After all, she (he) needs to acquaint herself with this reshaping of the property—choosing spots for personal tasks, along with inquiring whether small varmints might live below the surfaces. CHJICK'S present standard poodle, Maddie, was born a hunter, thus is equipped with exquisite senses of sight, smell and hearing. It is a joy to watch her stop, lift a front paw, cock her head, then jump two or three feet, pounce and dig, nose into a hole, perhaps to catch a mole or vole. Squirrels or chipmunks are always chased, seldom caught.

Clearing the forest growth covering rock outcroppings is beyond joyful. Rocks on the surface may appear to be disconnected. As you progress, however, pulling away vines, weed roots, and small bushes, a network of inter-related stone and rock reveals itself. The interactive formations are striking, well worth exploring and displaying. Part of the pleasure is identifying these intricate works of natural art are yours, to be viewed and enjoyed from the day of discovery forward.

<u>Brush Walls</u>. While working on the Wintergreen second lot CHUCK discovered a most useful addition to the property: the BRUSH WALL. Rather than removing limbs and other brush-like material, one is bound to find perfectly useful bordering substances. In tidying up downed limbs and collecting them over time, these items were placed and piled along the edges of the property as a brush wall. As it happened, the walls looked great, clearly designating the lot's boundaries.

Gradually, the walls increase in height, appearing as natural barriers edging the property. The walls will settle somewhat, resulting in branches re-positioning themselves and requiring maintenance, for example, trimming those sticking out of or over the wall. Not a problem, indeed a source of enjoyment, as with all natural caring activities. A tip: Pay attention to stabilizing the wall during its construction by inserting some branches vertically as you build. These vertical pieces create a network facilitating the steadiness as the wall grows in height. A very nice feature is the brush wall as border is never complete, thus encouraging its builder to monitor it on a regular basis. One can foresee in the future adding to the south wall to reach a height totally blocking out the neighbor's house. Maybe not. Just a thought.

Let's go inside now, perhaps to return to nature later. Chapter three will introduce and treat a wide variety of personal matters that either are familiar to you but may well take different form in retirement. The point is to review these features as they affect in their altered condition.

Chapter Three

Personal Care
(and related matters)

Attention now turns directly to you, focusing on rather bland every day issues: getting up in the morning or what to do when a body part hurts. CHUCK knows a lot about these ordinary matters. Understand, however, most of his experiences are personal and of limited relevance for you. So—what is offered can serve only as a basis for comparative analysis or as practices you find instructive. Bottom line: You can't lose and you may pick up useful hints or warnings.

<u>Arising and Meeting the Day</u>. Retirement is great, yet takes getting used to. It begins dramatically by your waking up in the morning. Guess what. You don't *have* to get out of bed, shave, comb whatever hair remains, brush those choppers, and dress in job clothes. You can roll over and luxuriate in bonus rest, perhaps turn on the radio and listen to the news or, better yet, restful music. Arise when you feel like it, step into slippers, fit yourself into a warm robe, run your fingers through your hair, and greet the day. If luck is on your side, you may smell bacon or sausage crackling, with a big farm breakfast to follow. Coffee, too, is waiting in

the cup, newspaper laid out nearby. Welcome to the retiree's world, maybe.

Perhaps, not this first day, but very soon, you will have obligations. There is a new life beyond breakfast. Open doors are limitless. Very likely you already have a list of projects in mind for this newly earned space and time. Sports, for example, golf, tennis, hiking, fishing, skiing, boating, to name a few, invite your attention. Gardening and lawn care are frequently required, along with home and garage repairs neglected in favor of career enhancement. It is hard to identify all possibilities. The point here is to urge advance planning, thinking through and creating an agenda.

CHUCK greets each day with many more activities in mind than can reasonably be managed through the day. And as it happens, working on one item uncovers other related tasks, especially the case for outdoor work and home maintenance. Do realize, however, immutable rules govern your options. Let's see, all activities take longer than anticipated, all tasks require tools you may not have, and you are certain to under estimate your capacity to take on these jobs. However, think of these realities as invigorating. Be positive, whatever that may mean. But give it a try.

Let's back up. If, for whatever reason, you have trouble sleeping, due perhaps to a dip in the stock market, an unfortunate political discussion with a neighbor, or your team having suffered an upset, turn your attention to your list of projects. Run through the items, evaluating each and asking what is needed to finish a job. The shift from what is irritating to what is bound to be satisfying will be relaxing. You can feel relief throughout your body, followed by restful sleep which prepares one to tackle the tasks. Try it. Can't hurt. A good night's sleep is basic to rewarding work. Consider some basics.

Exercise. Alas your body is flagging. That is the bad news, delivered daily. The good news is you can slow or postpone the decline. Really. Your first hurdle is accepting and acting on this good news. Next up is designing an exercise program, followed by carrying the program out, preferably daily. CHUCK found these tasks to be challenging. "Persevere," he concluded, finally settling on this maxim: *The less you want to exercise, the more you need to do it.* So, get off your butt and make that first move.

Your goal in an exercise program should be genuine guilt for missing those stretches, bends, twists, and contortions. When guilt replaces relief from postponing a set, you are on your way to positive effects for your body. Be patient. Muscles and joints will take time to adjust to new routines. Rather soon, however, your disciplined regularity will settle in as physical and mental adjustments are realized.

An exercise program mostly evolves over time. There are some guidelines however. Perhaps the most important suggestion for CHUCK was provided by a physical therapist with whom he worked following recovery from his first heart attack. Now there's a stimulus worth heeding. The therapist's first name was Vonda—easy to recall for CHUCK because his older sister was a nurse named Wanda. In their first meeting, Vonda explained exercise did not have to be hard work. She counseled the program should be regular, repetitive, and restrained. Put otherwise, the program should not be a test of one's manhood. Slow, steady, and daily were advised.

Several practices may be added to "Vonda's Basics." For example, keep a record on a daily calendar. On the exercise day, enter having done one's workout, along with other relevant health notes. CHUCK records the low temperature of the day, types of exercise, and special activities. He also plays music—a pleasant background to exercising. Watching television or videos is not recommended—too much of a diversion. But, of course, for some guys diversion is what they want. Still, not advised.

Count! Set a reasonable number for each exercise. CHUCK'S count for the stationary bike pedaling is a minimum of 300. However, he does several exercises while using the bike, each with its own count. Consider 30 each with weights, for chest pulls, elbow taps, and upper body stretches. True enough, counting is boring. But counting performs the useful function of signaling how close you are to finishing. And it keeps you on track, noting how far along you are.

Location? Home or fitness center? Inside? Outside? Each is a crucial decision. There are several advantages should you have space at home. You can select your equipment, avoid having to set a time and driving elsewhere, arranging and paying for a membership, and having to display your exercising profile in public. Needless to say, CHUCK chooses privacy over publicity. Another important plus is that you own your equipment. Check out a second-hand shop for your purchases. Used items are likely to be in good shape, having been barely broken in by the previous owner who may have quit real early.

True enough, many, possibly most, guys find the fitness center offers socializing experiences. CHUCK finds it to be a distraction from the purposes of exercise. If the trip and the social exchanges are motivating, go for it. Just don't let yakking with friends interfere with exercise.

Segmentation. A useful tip: Consider separating exercise segments through the day. Base the divisions on the purposes served. The advantages are to reduce the stress and strain of a lengthy workout and to suit individual goals.

CHUCK'S program offers a good example. He divides the program into three segments: (1) Following toilet activities and making the bed—place two pillows on a waist-high table or chest, bend over on the pillows, raise each leg in turn to a count of 20 to 25. (2) 11:00 a.m. Floor exercises, primarily yoga in nature and mostly variations in stretching. (3) 10-11 p.m. Working with exercise equipment (bike, foot swing, stand-on rocker, NordicTrack: walk fit and ski sets.

These three stages work well for his needs. The first gets his legs working after a night of rest, the second is a basic routine for the day, and the third, while at a late hour, aids in preventing cramps in bed. Combined the movements work all the joints and their daily actions support walking, stair climbing, and outdoor activities.

<u>Pills</u>. Most of CHUCK'S tablets are food, so designated by his holistic physician. Powdery for the most part, various mushrooms are encapsulated, aimed for different parts of the body. Often one swallows two, occasionally spitting one out as it gets caught in the throat. Unsurprisingly, cough ups are highly annoying. Your eyes can bulge. In another form, some capsules contain liquid in varying amounts, larger ones are definitely "coughupable." Take care. Additionally, as is evident in these remarks, one must organize pill taking through the day, then recall those timings. Easier said than done.

The prescription medications are likewise variable, served in dissimilar shapes for obvious reasons and softish so as to disintegrate swiftly into your throat. Perhaps spreading these pills through the day is best so as to avoid a big whack to the body all at once. Here is CHUCK'S routine: First set, mostly mushroom based, soon after rising; second set, to include prescriptions, around noon; third set, a mixed group, early evening. Does he sometimes forget a set? Absolutely. Recall at his age, he may have frequent memory lapses, and so might you along the way. Are the pills fulfilling their purposes? Hard to say. Easier just to trust the prescriber. Hopefully the number is limited, with few conflicts among them. Do consider the result, just had his 90th birthday and continues to arise in the morning feeling no worse than the day before. That is special and marks him as grateful. Do keep having birthdays a sensible goal.

Proper pill taking depends entirely on the patient. Develop a schedule and stick with it, bearing in mind those aging effects on memory. Nobody ever said any of these personal processes would be easy or lacking interactive effects.

Getting Help. Typically each passing year invites more help from others. Examples of functions needing outside help? Hearing, seeing, walking, shoveling, eating. We humans are astonishingly designed to manage on our own for decades. But, as the saying goes: "Stuff happens" to older folks. Whole trades have emerged to assist you, at a cost paid in large part through Medicare and supplementary insurance. Here is a sample.

Hearing. Your ears are intricate devices, remarkable but they can begin to fail as you age. You find yourself asking "what?" with greater frequency. For whatever reason you resist getting help. Hearing aid manufacturers understand this reluctance and have sought to make their products less visible. Alas, the more features they pack into their tiny devices the more obvious they become. Soon what is already one of the least attractive facial features comes to be an unattractive adornment. Furthermore, the device may pick up noise unwanted by the listener, as with competing conversations at a dinner party or whispers at a concert. Additionally, one of the aids emits a shrill whistle.

CHUCK is an experienced hearing aider. Reduced hearing showed up in his late 70s, continuing the unwelcome trend into his 80s. He resisted getting help to the annoyance of his wife and some friends. Finally he got tested and hearing aids were recommended. Get this: he asked if he could start with one ear only. A patient, if not a fully understanding, audiologist suggested two! They cost seven times his first car—a 1950 used, yet wholly reliable, Plymouth!! As he left the ear repair establishment with his new ears, he remarked to his wife: "It was a whole lot cheaper to ask 'what?'"

His first set operated with tiny batteries lasting roughly two weeks. He asked his wife to change the batteries—her slim fingers for his fat ones. He bought batteries by the dozens, tossing as trash some over 50 a year. Imagine how many million wearers were dumping tiny used batteries. Every six months CHUCK went to the audiologist to dry out the aids. At the visit, he was typically given a small pack of batteries for being a good boy.

Obviously this process came to be highly irritating. CHUCK and his wife, now joining him in the fun, bought new rechargeable hearing aids. They cost less than half of the first set and came with additional features, including a dry out box. One vital advisory: Make certain you remove the aids before showering or bathing. You may wonder how CHUCK discovered this cautionary suggestion. Further advice: Paste a note on the shower door or on the tub reading simply "EARS." Not foolproof but mostly works as a reminder. Hearing aids aren't in need of a scrubbing.

Vision. CHUCK got his first pair of glasses as a teenager. Adulthood has been a long established pattern of myopia requiring stronger and stronger lenses. Regular visits to optometrists and ophthalmologists have resulted in a long trail of new specs. Chances are very good that the reader has his or her own story, possibly for some folks accompanied by varieties of other eye diseases. Fact is any gathering will illustrate the dominance of vision correctives. A recent example: Last night in attending a dinner of sixteen people in our age range. All wore glasses.

How does one cope with deteriorating sight? Much depends, of course, on the importance of seeing clearly to your daily life. For CHUCK his eyes were critical for his work as a professor, essentially requiring reading and writing. Stylistic and mechanistic adjustments were necessary through the decades. Glasses are, of course, crucial, along with good strong ears to hold them in place. (Note: Contact lenses may also be placed directly on the eye, thus avoiding the "Mr. Magoo" profile).

Several methods may be utilized to aid sight. CHUCK has employed them all. (1) Primary among these aids is light. He sometimes uses head lamps in reading and making home repairs. For lectures he often clipped a lamp on the lectern to view his notes. When delivering public talks he first evaluated the lighting in the room. Often the talk was to be delivered from shadows. I kid you not. (2) Enlargement of notes was often necessary. The computer has been a huge benefit in offering a range of large fonts, as with No. 22, in preparing notes or manuscripts. (3) A magnifying glass has been a constant companion, notably given variation of type in printed material; likewise the color and brightness of the print itself varies. (4) Someone to help by reading small print. As CHUCK has aged reading has become more of a challenge and can be slow and tiring for the eyes. Often, his partner in life reads for him, and her. Their Standard Poodle curls up in front of the fireplace for the reading hour. (Note: New devices have been developed in recent years to aid those with limited vision.)

One difficult problem may not have to be identified for myopic older retired men as they have experienced it. The challenge is identifying the men's room in a restaurant or other public place. No problem if the rooms are identified as "Men" or "Women." The issue arises if figures are used or other words are substituted: "fellas" or "hombres" or "guys." The point is Mr. Magoo has to slap his face up close to the door to insure he gets in the correct rest room. Suffice it to say, CHUCK is well aware of this potential embarrasement.

It is common for your regular visit to the optometrist to recommend stronger lenses. One of CHUCK'S eye guys explained he could make him see better but he was unable to halt or reverse the downward trend line in sight. CHUCK'S vision would simply continue to worsen. As it happened, however, cataract surgery some years later dramatically improved his sight. Cataracts rank high on the list of eye ailments. Surgery can remove cataracts and insert new, clear lenses to improve sight. In CHUCK'S case removal restored the quality of his vision to what it was in his 30s. His thick and weighty glasses were replaced with thin and light units. With certain printed material he even could read without specs.

Five years past and his left eye weakened with cataract-like effects. His surgeon recommended laser surgery to remove the cloudiness, returning to the immediate post-surgery clarity. The procedure took some over two minutes. The result was exactly as described by the surgeon. Furthermore, the surgeon noted, the positive effect of the laser surgery was "forever," never having to be repeated. The method is referred to as "posterior capsulotomy."

Guess what? In 2022 the corrective laser surgery was completed for the right eye as it came to cloud up as well. The result was similar, a return of the clarity following cataract surgery. A miracle. As it happened, this laser surgery permitted the completion of the book CHUCK was writing.

Walking. Striding out is commonplace for most folks along the way to retirement. Soon, however, walking and running begin to demand special attention with further aging. On the one hand, such motions are recommended as exercise—the more the better in one's fitness program. Fortunately, the environment offers low-cost or no-cost places to walk and run. In most cases, one need only open the door and stride out.

CHUCK is a walker. He has had to be. Like so many of us, growing up was dominated by walking—to school, a job, meeting with friends, shopping, entertainment, dating. This universal mode of mobility promotes reassurance and security. Knowing a destination is walkable induces confidence. You can make it while benefiting from the exercise. In present times technology provides gimmicks which count one's steps. Actually you were always equipped, at no cost, to manage the task. It goes something like this: one, two, three…and so forth for each step. Wow. If you can count to 100 and recall how many 100s you have stepped, you are in business.

Running has become a popular pastime, a fine exercise. CHUCK ran competitively in high school—the mile, half-mile, and relays. He was not very good at it competitively but has saved his few third-place medals for no obvious reason. Having satisfied whatever urge led him to compete at a sub-par level he stopped racing forevermore. Not so for Brother Lou who ran for decades, to include marathons. Of course, Lou also was in the Marines—a prideful man. Brother Bob also ran competitively and in marathons, along with his sons.

Having given up competition, CHUCK did run memorably in January, 1975, on the occasion of the first Super Bowl win by the Pittsburgh Steelers. Following years of serving as the doormat of the National Football League the Steelers won the top prize. CHUCK and his two sons were so pumped up they had to do more than just celebrate inside. They put on running shoes and took to the streets, whooping and hollering. Not even Terry Bradshaw or Franco Harris could match their enthusiasm. The Steelers won three more Super Bowls in the next five years. But the first, Super Bowl IX, was the best for the Jones boys.

Private enterprise soon sought to benefit from the running fad. Seeking to profit sporting markets offer complete running wardrobes, along with proper foot wear. Some equipment, notably shoes and striding poles, are also available to walkers. Fact is, you can walk or run dressed in an old pair of shorts, a Tee-shirt, and past-their-prime tennis shoes. Also highly likely, however, your neighbors will be decked out in the sports store attire. Choice is yours. Important point is the exercise itself.

Shoveling. CHUCK and Vera now live in the mountains, the beautiful Blue Ridge Mountains of Virginia. Their home is located some over 3,000 feet. It snows at that level. Indeed, in winter it is often cold enough to manufacture snow for ski runs. When natural snow falls it drops on his driveway and his many pathways. Hooray. Snow removal is a chance for a truly useful exercise.

How prepared is CHUCK to start shoveling? By count he has two standard shovels, one wide shovel, a couple of ice chippers, a wide push broom two regular sized sweepers, and a half dozen digging implements. In other words, standard snow removal tools for a guy born in South Dakota and living in Wisconsin. Take note, however, none of these instruments were created by their owner. That honor belongs to the McPlow, a home-crafted device. Pray tell, what Is a McPlow?

Listen up recent retirees. Few things are as satisfying as creating a practical tool. Here is how CHUCK started. He ordered a small plow on wheels online. On arrival he found it would not do the job of clearing the driveway. The wheels were plastic and much too small. The handle came in two parts with a small snap to hold the two sections together. The steel plow itself was strong enough but the mechanism was too weak to actually move snow. Result? A good idea poorly executed.

Fortunately the mountain resort has a dumpster where neighbors often leave useable items no longer needed. It was there CHUCK spotted exactly the device for transforming his online reject into a working McPlow. The find was a 1950s golf bag holder with large wheels—nearly bicycle size. The online plow was nested into the cart secured with nearly a large roll of duct tape. The McPlow works effectively, pushes up to 5 inches of snow. It operates with one hand directing the cart. This winter will be its 12th season of plowing. And, as it happened, 20221-2022 has been the most challenging ever for the McPlow, even requiring additional duct tape.

A cautionary note: Alas, snow in the mountains of the Blue Ridge is not limited to 5 inches. Occasionally the snow drop may be 10 inches or more. In the last decade storms produced up to 20 inches, once leaving more than 30 inches piled up against the garage door. What to do as the McPlow remained quietly snuggled in its place inside the garage?

The answer? A giant born and raised in Maine arrived with a serious plow attached to the front of a pickup truck. Matt, by name, and his equally sizeable son, removed the snow from the driveway. If you live in the mountains and don't have such a service, find a Matt and pay them well.

Eating. A life-long function comes to be magnified even more for recent retirees. What has settled into standard practices typically is transformed for you and your mate.

Additionally how and what you eat comes to take a central role in maintaining good health.

Let's start with probing these questions: Who's cooking? Has the new presence in the kitchen, you, taken over? Who was the chef before retirement? Was it already a cooperative food preparation practice? The point is how much change may we expect? And finally, did job isolation at home during the pandemic provide a practice run on these arrangements?

Equally important is the household timing for eating. What is the schedule and how might it change with a new presence? Age-old practices commonly divided eating into three segments: breakfast, lunch, and dinner. Let's call it the 1-2-3 method. Typically the first and third meals were at home. Lunch was at or near the work place. This timing has changed dramatically, often determined by a wide variety influences. You, the recent retiree, have to get fed in whatever pattern has developed. Could be you have to fend for yourself, eating whenever and whatever. The 2020 pandemic scrambled eating patterns also, all across the nation and beyond.

At 90, CHUCK was able for the most part to continue practices set decades before. Fortunately his partner, Vera, was also schooled in the 1-2-3 method. Put otherwise, they made few dietary changes in retirement and subsequently to the present. Adjustments included the breakfast menu, timing of the evening meal, and more frequent meals out.

As mentioned before personal notes are illustrative only, not a recommendation for the reader. This caution is notably relevant in regard to eating. Given the substantial variation in personal and family habits, a recent retiree is advised only to be sensitive to his or her more regular presence in household patterns. Be attentive to existing routines.

More Personal Issues. This general topic is expansive and yet variable among individual retirees. Scent and dress are especially relevant to retirees as associated with their post-job lives. Take notice.

Scent. In large part how and if you smell can vary over time. During his youth, CHUCK carried the aroma of LIFEBUOY soap. A British perfumed product developed by Lever Brothers was popular during the post-World War II period. As a guy's cleansing agent, "Lifebuoy" projected the manliness of an athlete, even for a skinny kid.

As a teen and beyond to the 20s special occasions, dating for example, required scenting more upscale, perhaps with a splash of OLD SPICE following a shave. More costly, of course, but whereas Lifebuoy smelled showery Old Spice offered more—a sweet longer-lasting whiff and a signal of shaving.

It became evident during military service and subsequently in graduate work at the University of Wisconsin that CHUCK'S body mostly didn't stink. Apart from passing wind occasionally, he was "good to go" socially. What a relief. A daily shower or bath scrub suited to neutralize any unpleasant body smells. Deodorants came to be unused as unnecessary, but were kept on the ready.

So, as with most men (I suspect), CHUCK sailed through his mature life smelling clean or perhaps just neutral. Oh, keeping those choppers sparkling and one's breath fresh as a mint were also required. Retirement typically changes social and professional life accompanying a job. The retiree's personal world changes with a move out of work. Adjustments are required, perhaps including one's scent.

Let's think about this new world. Could well be friends and neighbors change. Some may move elsewhere, others spending winter months in Florida or other warmer spots. Same is true for you and your partner. Time has its effects— little may change early on, then gradually relationships are altered. Will those still with jobs find the new you compatible? Or if you move south or someplace close to the kids, how might you fit into the new location? How likely are you to be accepted regularly dressed in shorts, Tee-shirt, no socks, and sandals? And, with aging, do you detect an obvious tendency for OMO?

Managing OMO (Old Man's Odor) is tricky. It can creep into your body unbeknown to its carrier. The source? It could be naturally hidden in the wrinkles of age. Perhaps it shows up in one's clothes. Or simply the effects of fewer regular scrubbing downs. The reality seems to be: The older you get, the more apparent OMO is, yet the less it is apparent to the aging man.

General advice? Be sensitive to this natural order of scent. Try what makes sense to you but don't turn yourself into a flower.

<u>Dress</u>. The retiree's closet is likely to be chockful of work clothes, some of which may be uniforms. Many, perhaps most, clothes are kept clean. Those items closely associated with the job, e.g., a police, military, or hospital uniform, are unlikely ever again to be worn. In a manner of speaking, however, a suit, shirt, and tie may also be so designated, as can a sports coat, shirt, and tie. The point is clothing often is identified with the nature of work, thus no longer commonly usable as daily attire.

For the most part, a fresh retiree is free to dress however he or she feels comfortable. There is no common "stay at home" wardrobe. Some fellas have been known to wear all day what they had on when they tumbled out of bed, much to the annoyance of their partner. Others slip on a comfortable robe as they settle into a favorite chair with their morning coffee. More likely, however, is the selection of clothing related to plans for the day. Whatever the choice, the retiree begins a process of reconfiguring what is to be worn.

A systematic approach to dressing differently is forward looking, that is to say planning ahead. What are you likely to be doing in retirement? Even slouching requires thought.

CHUCK has settled on a wardrobe adaptable to his retiree standard activities. Easiest to resolve were the trousers. Blue jeans fit the bill. Rather rapidly he came to appreciate the tractability of jeans, suiting as they do almost any upper body dress, notably either shirts or jackets. Accordingly, he keeps a half dozen or so jeans, varying only slightly in shades of blue.

What about the top? CHUCK is a Tee-shirt kind of guy, commonly changing every other day. Sweaty work calls for a daily switch. A quick sniff in the pits signals the need either to change or to give the under shirt another day. As for the outer shirt, select three or four favorites, making a switch every two to three days. Air the shirt out for a couple of days and you may be able to put it back to work later. These routines come to be your life fella. Get used to them.

Pockets! Useful as they are, jeans are typically limited to four pockets. Often an activity calls for more, larger, and possibly with secure flaps. Cargo pants are useful in this regard, notably by providing roomy pockets above the knees. Also useful is a light jacket with large pockets. Similarly a carpenter's apron with categorized pocketry may be essential for building and/or repair projects. CHUCK is definitely pro-pocket, even in dress-up clothes. He warns, however, one can forget what is in each pocket. Furthermore, memory declines with aging. So items may get lost in the personal world of pockets.

<u>Creams and Such</u>. You will accumulate more and more creams as you age, partially stimulated by the inevitable process of moving from your vigorous life as a working stiff to an old and yet older guy. Let's imagine you are now in your 80s. Your cream- or jell-like substances may range from the always reliable Vaseline to a modern tube of Preparation H, with a dozen or so other jars and tubes. Distinguishing among them comes to be important, even vital, along with your pills.

CHUCK offers several recommendations of soothing and curing creams as illustrative only, understanding, of course, any guy's set is related to his personal prescriptions.

<u>Vaseline.</u> Advertised as "Original Healing Jelly" this item is a must, and likely is in your bathroom already, perhaps also in the garage or work place. Applications are diverse: rough spots, wounds, sores, burns, feet, hair, a "go to first" jelly. It may also be used as a lubricant on squeaky door hinges, stubborn locks, and household tools.

<u>Udderly Smooth Body Cream.</u> This cream is a dream. Developed for hand milking cow teats, it works beautifully on your feet, smoothing the cracks and rough spots. CHUCK discovered it at Ace Hardware. Being bald, he also applies it occasionally to his head with impressive results. It has a light and pleasant aroma.

<u>Vitamin E Skin Care Cream.</u> A marvelous spread. Apply to face, hands, arms, back. A pleasant odor. Widely available. CHUCK gets it at Walmart where it is sold in a two-jar packet. Applied daily after a bath or shower, you will have a fresh odor through the day—a most friendly cream.

<u>Nivea Crème</u>. This product is a serious, thick application—manly in nature. It simply does not meld easily into your skin. Rub it in. You know you are wearing it. As the saying goes: "It has shoulders." A German creation one has to dig fingers into the crème and slap it on the site, then spread it evenly. It is made to last. Indeed, even a small container will be with you the rest of your life.

<u>Spring Wind.</u> Referencing creams with muscles, as with Nivea, Spring Wind comes to mind. Somehow "cream" doesn't quite capture its tough character, nor does its label. Dark brown in color and as thick as Nivea, this balm goes to work on any pain anywhere. Try it on a sore knee or ankle. CHUCK is presently applying it to aches in his toes. Caution alert: The ointment can stain clothing as it performs its dirty duties.

<u>Vick's VapoRub.</u> No stains here but definitely fits in the "tough as nails" category of balms. My neighbor will never apply it as it is associated for him with his youth when his mom kept his chest slathered in Vicks. The strong analgesic odor has stayed with him for decades. Surely not the balm to

apply before attending a cocktail party. Your scent precedes you into any room. But there is no denying its effectiveness for suppressing a cough, as it has over the decades.

Tubes: A huge variety of applications are produced in tubes. The cream-like contents are created for specific purposes. No surprise then that a run-of-the-mill guy collects several tubes over time. Here is a sample:

Neo-Sporin. An antibiotic ointment useful for cuts and bruises. A must for the active, yet naturally clumsy, aging retiree.

Cortizone 10. Old guys tend to start itching in various places—waist, ankles, underarms, wrists, etc. Gets worse as you age. C-10 to the rescue. Don't run out or you will go mad.

Lotrimin.AF. An antifungal, typically used for athlete's foot and related discomforts. Many alternatives for this product, as most readers are aware from being introduced to it from high school sports.

Preparation H ointment. A hemorrhoid treatment for which you will be forever in debt. Apply it generously. Keep a fresh tube handy. The manufacturer also sells a "cooling gel." Very nice. However, do not make the mistake of expecting it will work like the ointment. The two are packaged much the same, save for the cap: dark for the ointment, white for the gel. That kind of clue is why you "Ask CHUCK."

That's it for personal matters. Apologies for any items with which you are already well acquainted. In my home town a familiar response to advice from others is "I knew that before you know." Furthermore, there is a great deal CHUCK does not know, thus leaving you on your own.

Chapter Four

Enjoying Life: Live as You Dwindle

This book has directed the reader's attention to important changes later in your life. Drawing on CHUCK'S experience I will in this last chapter review several topics associated with these changes. There will be a new you, a retired you, a reformed you, perhaps a new job you. For the most part retirement is presented positively, at least in the short run.

In the long stretch, however, retirement is a declaration of aging, typically bearing numbers like 65 and beyond. How long will the good times last? It is truly hard for any one individual to determine. Therefore planning can be difficult. For the fact is aging during retirement years is a process of departure as measured by you and others, notably family, friends, colleagues, neighbors, associates, and those in the "and so forth" category. The longer you hang around, the more likely fading will occur. Your body informs you what is happening as this or that part flags or stops working all together, to include eyes, ears, hands, feet, knees, back—you get the idea. Others also view your decline. "CHUCK just doesn't seem himself anymore." Or "You can't rely on old CHUCK anymore." Hmmmm…

Aging as a process of departure requires a bit of management on your part. As suggested, not so much in its early stages. But over time the process can encourage a rather sour disposition as the years pile up. CHUCK'S advice is to beat back temptations for adverse attitudes and find ways to enjoy life. In other words, *live as you dwindle*. Showing how is the purpose of this chapter. The notion was nicely summarized in a headline in a *Wall Street Journal* book review: "Might As Well Be Glad." (March 5, 2022, p. C12) So true. Conditions of decline are stark, depressing, and frontline. You have nothing to lose by being happy. Try it. "Might as well." It's free and, by the way, mostly quite hilarious. I will show you how, beginning with managing the dwindling process in your favor.

Socializing: There is so much to discuss on this topic that I will focus only on those matters CHUCK has identified as seriously amusing. First, remember the older you get the more likely you are to get scratched from a host's list of invitees. "So and so is giving a party and we weren't invited." Should you still be listed, perhaps with a question mark, certain guidance is helpful.

Much socializing is done STANDING in crowded settings or, following drinks, sitting at the dinner table. Basically standing is not good for old folks. Your feet start to ache, then your new knees, followed by your artificial hip. Get near a place to sit, perhaps an arm chair or sofa back. You may risk, of course, getting stuck with a person also seeking relief from standing and this person could well be a deadly dull cocktail conversationalist. Not good and possibly not funny.

CHUCK tells me he has a solution to this problem. Real cases in point: (1) The conversationalist is describing in detail the installation of his new home generator. (2) Another talker is reconstructing his early dating with his eventual wife. Interrupt either person mid-story and ask: "Would you hold my drink, please?" Each agrees—hard to turn down a "please." CHUCK then bends over to the floor and touches his toes, while turning his head up to smile. Popping back up, he retrieves his drink from a stunned talker and limps off. CHUCK reports he once received applause for this move. Try it, if you can still touch your toes.

Let's turn more directly to your behavior as a participant socializer. It could well be, of course, that you are not a cocktail conversationalist. No need to be, as many party-goers are super happy to have listeners, even if glassy-eyed. However, should you decide to join a conversation there are some rules for those in their 80s. As the age clock ticks, memory may well slip. Before speaking, review how likely it is you can get through a story. Have a couple of synonyms on the ready for those words or phrases you may have forgotten. A similar rule applies for names you have lost—think of how to identify a person without calling the name. And here is a general guideline: Keep your contribution brief. Your listeners will appreciate the effort though some may well take advantage of a break to take charge—they are referred to as "sentence finishers." So, speak as fast as you can to prevent being interrupted. Good luck with that if you are in your eighties!

A dinner party can be challenging in many ways for the older set. There is the non-verbal problem of eating cleanly. CHUCK comes to the rescue once again. Handling utensils requires nimble fingers you may no longer possess. Fumbling digits (see "hands" below) may fill your lap with portions of your dinner. Potential solution? Move your plate partially off the table covering a portion of your lap, coincident with snuggling your chair up closer to the table. CHUCK reports these actions work most of the time for re-plating food, say, peas, beans, mushrooms, salad items, even cake crumbs. Furthermore, the host and hostess will be grateful for your failure to drop food on the floor from your lap when you stand to leave. Doing so could prevent your being "de-listed," not to mention the awkwardness of your assuming the crawl position to pick up the floored food—at your age?.

Hosting: Among the changes accompanying aging is fewer dinner parties hosted by senior citizens. There are several reasons for this development, primarily explained by "we're just not up to it anymore." The chef can't face feeding a large table of hungry, besotted folks. The bar tender doesn't trust pouring drinks during the cocktail hour or wine at dinner time. To do so gives a whole new meaning to the term "Hand Shake." Hire someone or recruit one of the younger guests to help. And neither host or hostess may feel up to leading dinner talk. See the risks discussed in "socializing" above.

What to do? Bowing out only confirms the dwindling process. So the positive social approach suggests reducing the number invited, perhaps two—a couple of good friends. Another method is hosting one or more couples at a favorite restaurant. This second option is most appealing— no vacuuming before or setting the table, serving drinks, preparing food, filling the dishwasher, and, very critical, anticipating when the guests will leave.

Conclusion on hosting? Surely worth doing. Possibly inviting those near your ages. BUT if you can, do work on maintaining contact with younger folks. Doing so may remind you of your own youth. Probably best, however, to let them do most of the talking. Limit your participation to brief comments supporting a guest's story.

Generations: As a retiree you will be moving through phases of generational change. These periods have definite effects as you progress to the top of the family tree. In the early stages you may well still have Moms and Dads. One or both may even have moved in with you and your partner or live close by, possibly in an elder care facility. The arrangements are diverse but the effects may be standardized as in providing a measure of care. Thus as you are managing adjustments to joblessness, a portion of your time is scheduled for meeting the needs of aging parents. How that works case-by-case is beyond simply acknowledging the dissimilarity of restrictions imposed. Best of luck. And do learn from the experience as lessons to be applied when you both have moved to that same position.

More relevant is how you handle easing into top -of-the-tree status. CHUCK'S experience was free of direct care of either his parents or those of his in-laws. Sisters and brothers managed his parents and good health and independence provided strength for his spouse's parents. Consequentially, retirement was not accompanied by serious restrictions associated with parental care. More attention was paid to relating to their children and grandchildren. Positive incentives encouraged freshness in interactions with those down the generational ladder substituting for potential adverse inducements associated with advanced aging. A lesson here? I think so. Whatever your case, look for the more positive option so as to preserve an optimistic life as you join the parade of family working their way through levels of aging.

Decorating: Holidays and seasonal changes are among the most uplifting occasions for retirees. Typically these are times of family gatherings, often at the home of the most senior members. CHUCK is a decorator and has, over the years developed the ways and means for brightening their home in a manner suiting the event— Christmas, New Year's, Easter, Independence Day, and Fall. He specializes on Christmas and Fall, yet is sensitive to the other celebratory occasions as well.

Having practiced the decorating craft for decades tends to refine one's expertise, thus legitimizing advice-giving. At the top of the "what to do" list are categorization and storing of the accumulation of holiday and fall items. Mark and store key objects for upcoming events. The Fall, in particular, invites themes. The blessed pumpkin is vital, both in plastic and even more in its natural beauty as a live vegetable. So pumpkins merit first in line discussion.

CHUCK recommends designing and displaying your autumn decorations in mid-October through Thanksgiving. At that point, save your pumpkins until Christmas, if possible. Garage them out of the sun, most can last as they soften up— just right for the following post-Christmas entertainment. Take your now near-squishy collection to an overlook nearby, preferably one with rocks below. Line them up and invite grandkids and their parents to throw them down on the rocks. There is a name for this process: A pumpkin "smoosh." CHUCK has managed this event for over 15 years. Note: Do go down to the rocks after the smoosh and toss the remains out of sight into crevices. Just remember; "A clean overlook is a virtuous overlook. Keep it that way"

Decorating for Autumn is absolutely delightful. Colors are incredible. CHUCK gets his big pumpkins at Walmart, the smaller ones at local farmers or merchants for a total of some over 20. Add a few gourds and several dried garden flowers and stalks to the decor, along with fern and other grasses. One gets excited just reminiscing about this autumn exercise and display. I guarantee passersby will compliment you for the show. We are talking major positive retiree feedback here.

On to Christmas and New Year's. You are more likely already to have a standard set of decorative items for this holiday event. Lights are, of course, featured. For whatever reason, however, the lights die during storage and must be replaced. Cutting the tree is always a delightful event, one missed by those buying trees cut or manufactured by others. Little joy to be had there. We have had friends buy cut trees, decorate them, then watch the needles fall off before Christmas. A pathetic sight. And let's be honest. Manufactured trees just don't make it, even if having been sprayed with pine smell.

Do think about personalizing your decorations, created just by you for the family. One item now firmly established in CHUCK'S family is a stump cut from the bottom of the previous year's tree. Initials of those attending are marked on the stump along with the year. Some over 20 stumps are spread in front of the fireplace each year. Lots of memories triggered there.

Other personalizing practices include family décor from the past. Perhaps you have saved items created by your children appropriate for hanging on the tree or placed by the fireplace. Special collections deserve display in the holidays, as with those of presidents from the White House historical office. Christmas and holiday cards can and should be incorporated into the spread. Make them available for family and friends to review. CHUCK'S family places them along the steps going upstairs. Do this display while holiday cards still arrive in the mail. Alas those arriving electronically aren't displayable, nor should they be.

The Christmas season ages along with you. The tree gets smaller as you start to shrink. Not that long ago CHUCK'S tree was over 10 feet high; now it is 6 to 8 feet high and placed on a coffee table. The unsteady, even treacherous, step ladder remains garaged. Lighting used to be both outside and inside, now only inside on the tree and limited. Additionally the starting date for holiday decorations keeps moving closer to December 25 as the decorator settles further into his or her 80s. Coincident with delay of the starting date is conversation among northern retirees about a couple of weeks in Florida during the holidays, much fun as it was to decorate for the grandkids—all now adults. Sadly advanced age sometimes can be lonely.

<u>Music</u>: This topic, too, is about enjoying life. As it happens, however, at least two features of music make it difficult to generalize. First and foremost is range, that is, its growth, and variability. Consequentially, what is sublime for one set of listeners turns others to screech in pain. Second, identifying "music I like," for example, "classical" will break out in a wide range of categories. The point is the most CHUCK can offer is to stress the roles music can play for the retiree in making adjustments in his life.

Let's begin with how it is delivered. CHUCK was born into a world of AM radio and scratchy pre-vinyl records. The radio delivered news, events, weather, sports, and drama into your home. Music tended to suit regional tastes. What that meant in eastern South Dakota, where he was born and lived as a young teen-ager, were mixes of country music on WNAX, Yankton. In the 1940s a Sioux Falls station (KELO perhaps) began playing classical music at five minutes before noon. CHUCK listened every day to a short piece or a movement of a larger piece.

FM radio stations then emerged in the daytime. Needing to fill the dial, classical music from vinyl records was played, typically with no advertising. Soon live musical performances were broadcasted. Furthermore, radios were installed in autos and computers stored endless musical styles and variants. Now retirees can fill their homes, autos, ear pieces, speakers, and other broadcasting devices with their music of choice.

Additionally flash drives can be designed to play personal choices of music.

Why play music? Why not? It can be both soothing and enlivening. It provides the perfect background for the lonesome retiree. Music will stimulate the imagination, which is precisely what retirement requires following the daily demands of routines associated with or even defining a job. Extra tip: As you slip into bed at night, turn on the radio, at a low level, to a favorite station. Sleep will soon follow. Many folks leave the radio on through the night. Take note: You cannot have too many radios. Count the number of rooms in your home, condo, tent, or wherever you are living out your retirement. Have a minimum of one radio in each sizable room.

Hands: As those days of dwindling progress, very likely in the late 70s and into the 80s, one's hands start to give out. It could be earlier, depending on your life's work. CHUK'S paternal grandfather managed a grain elevator and farm feed store. In his late 60s the tough and rough fingers started to curl into his hands. He would lift 100 pound feed bags by hooking his hands into the corners of the bags to place them into a pickup truck. Special note: During the post-World War II period wives often joined their husbands to choose patterns as the bags carried designs for making towels, children's blouses, pillow cases, and the like.

As a teenager, CHUCK worked his hands hard—helping his grandfather, in a separate feed store and a lumber yard managed by his uncle, on farms cutting weeds in corn rows, setting pins in a bowling alley, and delivering newspapers. However, for a vocation he chose a profession, teaching, unlikely to toughen those digits. Yet his hands were bound to harden sooner or later, as they likely will with you. With him, the hands began to weaken in his middle 80s.

The thumbs more than the other digits became less reliable. As it happens, these guys are the power units on the hands. They become less flexible, thus less dependable in powering the fingers to grip. You gradually lose the force of your hand as the thumb becomes stiff and misshapen. Okay for the left hand but for the sizable majority of right-handers, that thumb weakening makes it difficult to manage ordinary daily activities. Here is some of what may happen: buttoning shirts becomes a daily challenge, top button next to impossible. Using ordinary eating utensils is increasingly difficult—left thumb of little or no help. Many household tasks are difficult or simply impossible to accomplish.

Perhaps topping the list of ordinary skills or activities would be writing. The thumb turns out to have critical control in the multi-faceted function of handwriting. The skill required for holding and directing a pencil or pen comes to be more taxing as the thumb weakens. Fortunately other instruments aid in permitting the fingers to write, notably the computer, which also saves and provides storage for what you have written. Still even signing one's name, with a date, can be challenging.

Let's hear it for the thumb, this noblest of digits. It is sad to have to recognize its mainline function during late retirement. At the very least, however, the thumb deserves your attention earlier in case some exercise or treatment can prolong its utility for you as you dwindle otherwise. Oh, and by the way, try making your bed without your thumbs! If you discover a method, short of surgery, let CHUCK know.

Sports: Moving from a small topic, thumbs, to a gigantic subject, sports, requires spot-on emphasis. The focus here is simple: the role of sports in the life of a retiree. That function derives from how each individual views sports to be in his life.

CHUCK classifies two forms of sports: fandom and involvement. He recommends holding on as long as possible in each quest. As a fan you will have, over the years, established a set of commitments to individuals and teams, likely associated with where you live and the teams you follow. CHUCK lived in Pittsburgh during the 1970s. Result? A Steeler and Pirate fan forever. Meaning? Later he moved to Madison, Wisconsin, where he became a Green Bay Packer and UW Badger fan, along with renewing support for the Chicago Cubs in baseball. (Note: Normally fans stay with a team if they move, which can lead to mixed loyalties if the two teams play one another. To illustrate, the Steelers and Packers played each other in Super Bowl XLV in 2011. Packers won, barely. Still, either way, CHUCK would win.)

Staying with CHUCK'S teams for individual examples, Terry Bradshaw (Steelers) and Roberto Clemente (Pirates) represented his "heroes" in the 70s; Brett Favre and Arron Rodgers (Packers) and Ernie Banks (Cubs) met that standard in Wisconsin. By the way, the Cubs example drops back to high school days when the Cubs were the only major league baseball team whose games were broadcast by a Sioux Falls radio station.

One can begin to comprehend the complexity of the personal worlds of sports with this single case. Hopefully CHUCK'S case offers the justification for retaining the reader's own experiences. Guys like talking about "their" sports world so there is a conversationalist population for each pf CHUCK'S fan units, the Steelers, Packers, pirates, and so forth. These personal choices must remain active for the retiree, a way of staying in the game, so to speak, as otherwise you are slipping away.

The same holds for the second sports practice, your personal involvement. Whether it be golf, tennis, bowling, hunting, hiking, skiing, shooting baskets in a hoop on the garage, or any of dozens of other sporting endeavors, the activity is likely to be the source of social interaction, including friendly conversing, mostly. Hang on to the activity as long as your body will allow. It provides contact for possibly a couple of decades. Skiing was CHUCK'S family "involvement" sport. CHUCK kept with it until he was 88, Vera to 85. Both sons taught skiing for several years. Sports sustain life while you are departing. Even the aches sports produce personally remind you of the best life offers. It is hard to over stress this point. Stay with it fellas. Trust CHUCK on this, as if you needed to be so advised!

Travel: Here is where there likely will be a distinction between early retirement and later years. At first one is ready to hit the road—traveling to those places postponed precisely due to demands of a job. You have been set free and often the list of destinations is long. So break out the maps (what are those?) and flight schedules. Off to Europe, Hawaii, Africa, the Caribbean, Far East, and National Parks. All are ready and you will meet many of your compatriots doing the same.

Aging may slow you down as traveling wears you down. By the time you reach 85 home will be more comforting than airports in London or Paris. Your tolerance for delayed or cancelled flights will have run out. In fact your capacity to read the posted flight information may have diminished—CHUCK'S surely did. One consequence may be limiting travel to domestic sites. "How about we drive?" The pandemic surely encouraged domestic travel.

We now enter another realm of travel with its own set of issues. Eyes and ears are essential for safe driving, along with keen sensitivity to surroundings. These features are not uniformly sharp among an aging population. It is fair to observe as folks age, the less prepared they are to drive. Lengthy vacation trips are demanding and often tiring. Couples have the advantage of two drivers. Pared to one driver, however, creates uncertainties, suggesting eliminating lengthy trips. CHUCK no longer drives, due primarily to limited sight. As his wife concluded some years ago: "It is best to have the driver be the person who sees best." Sensible advice. An additional benefit? She drives very well.

In summary, travel for those in advanced age (85+) should be carefully evaluated for the risks involved. True enough, public transportation is available, to include limo services. But serious planning is required among senior citizens.

<u>Pets Always:</u> CHUCK and his wife of 63 years, Vera, have regularly had pets as family members. First was a remarkable black cat named "Bear," who lived with them for 18 years. He was joined by a black Labrador mix ("Tig") in 1963. The two were pals from Tucson to Pittsburgh, to Palo Alto, back to Pittsburgh where they both died the same year, 1975, to be buried beside one another along the garden wall. CHUCK and Vera's sons lived those years with Bear and Tig. Subsequently, they had dogs, in this order: Abby (German Shepherd),

Bonnie (Standard Poodle), Jude (Australian Shepherd), and Maddie (Standard Poodle—present dog). They also had a second cat—Timmy, Timmy (always pronounced twice) who also lived 18 tears.

CHUCK once joked that Vera was vital to the family so as to take care of his animals. The fact is he dearly loved each one. They all were vital to the family. Along the way the resident pets accompanied CHUCK, Vera, and the boys in the early years as they all traveled in their camper truck throughout the country. What rich and rewarding memories to replay in retirement.

The Color Purple: We have saved this last item for a nasty feature of an aging life: purple markings on CHUCK'S body. The color is attractive enough but not decorating his skin. Old guys tend to bump into solid objects—doors, railings, furniture, and the like. Purple marks show up, mostly on their arms but they can appear elsewhere as well. Not to worry, really, these spots are only blood under the skin but what is otherwise a nice color is unsightly on your arms and hands.

CHUCK has a solution of sorts, not foolproof but worth considering. Start by spotting those areas most vulnerable to purple blotches. Take an old pair of socks, cut off the tops, fold one top into the other and slide it the "bumper sock" up the vulnerable arm section. Elbows appear to be most susceptible. Good job. The sock tops will cushion the spot resisting all but the most severe whack. Sorry not much to aid the hands which in any event tend to get discolored on their own with age. You might try soft work t gloves but, hey, the youngest grandkids are likely to find your hands an intriguing rainbow of colors as is, so live with them.

<u>Weather.</u> Think back 30 or so years. Your parents are writing or calling, communicating in some manner. "Dad says it looks like rain but with this cold weather it could snow. Your mother and I are prepared. Don't worry about us." You both laugh. "They never check in with us without giving a weather report."

Now is now and both of you are fixated on weather. Typically each of you check the weather report first in the morning and talk about it over breakfast. Additionally, you both check the temperature through the day. Furthermore you attribute malice to the weather person if the day is cloudy, threatening rain, likely ruining your plans.

Nothing much you can do about this age-related obsession. It being a universal phenomenon, most of your friends will be weather bugs and content to visit with you. Just one note of caution: Be wary of those neighbors who have gone electronic and have transformed space upstairs into a weather central packed with equipment. As an old-fashioned "finger to the wind" devotee you will be overwhelmed.

<u>Reminiscences: A Note From CHUCK.</u> He was sitting in his favorite rocking chair in front of the fireplace thinking about his life and how it played out. The central topic came to be those people who, along the way, had a profound impact on him. He began to reminisce about these folks, moving along through the decades. The story began to tell itself. He decided to write it himself.

Greetings! The purpose of this segment is to encourage the reader to try this same mind game, exploring your journey in terms of those critical to your trip. It was fun, and often hilarious.

We start with Pa and Ma Jones, my paternal grandparents— Oscar Benjamin and Ruby Belle. Get this: When I ran away from home at age 12, they took me in. They were not looking for another son, they had 5, and one daughter, all adults with children. Pa told me when I graduated from college: "We will always think of you as our son." They were loving parents for a needy child.

Their daughter, Jeanette (called "Girlie") married a professor in my college. They and their family were my home in those years, forever to be comforting. Two others, "Doc" Farber and Pat Patterson, provided inspirational and intellectual stimulus then and forever more. Pat, now at 90 like me, was my role model throughout our lives. Both shared decades of professoring influencing dozens more like them.

Like most young men in the mid-1950s I served in the military. Army General Percy W. Clarkson commanded a joint task force in the Marshall Islands. I served humbly to this World War II veteran as his Army aide-de-camp. Army Lt. Colonel Fred Massey would impress any shave tail second Lieutenant, like me. Having received 7 purple hearts, he wore several bullet wounds and other scars on his back, shoulders, and legs. I once watched him toss a poker player out of the tent for cheating. These were guys who "did the job."

Another such guy was Lou Jones, my brother who joined the Marine Corps. After his service he became a business manager for Caterpillar, Inc. Alas, I didn't grow up with Lou, having left home. But we started to connect in the 1980s, becoming adult brothers from then to now. He fits well into the "do the job" category. In retirement he polished his skills as a poet, winning major awards for his writing. For me, he wins my ENVY AWARD. PS: He did not go to college, having schooled himself beyond institutional learning.

Following our military service, Pat Patterson and I lacked the graduate education for college teaching and research. "Doc" Farber advised us to attend the University of Wisconsin-Madison, completing our PHD's in three years. Professor Leon Epstein guided our way, while displaying how to use the degree in practice, as a role model for each of us.

Students at Wellesley College, my first job, taught me the basics of teaching them. They didn't realize what they were contributing, actually I probably hid it from them but their excellence led the way for me to engage their intelligence. Not hard for me to name one as extra special: Nora Ephron. Her capacity naturally to meld knowledge and humor was unsurpassed. That talent showed up in her outstanding career. What fun it was to learn from her and the classmates.

Got but this is fun!!

I wanted to follow Nora with someone who was her exact opposite, Holbert Carroll by name. A professor at the University of Pittsburgh, Bert was a calm, gentle, effective, and cooperative partner to me in managing the top journal in political science. He served as the book review editor. We lunched together frequently, resolving every question evenly and objectively. The most emotion he showed was a small smile. Time with Bert settled the tea, so to speak.

What could I learn from a Mom of two teenage boys while editing a major journal? As it turned out, a great deal. Kendall S. Stanley served as secretary, editorial assistant, and overseer of the journal process. Her orienting perspective was simple: "Get the journal published." That meant managing the articles and book reviews, alongside dealing with the scores of authors. Meanwhile she was in charge of her family. She put me in awe on a daily basis, supplemented with advice on how to manage my job. Impressed?

While in Pittsburgh, one must write about William J. Keefe. He chaired the department he had built. It was done with a permanent overlay of humor. To watch him manage was rewarding in many ways. Bill did not know any other way. There had been a demand in the department for more meetings. So as Bill and three other colleagues were in the Men's Room, Bill announced: "This counts as a meeting!" All agreed. One year the state legislature was at an impasse on the budget. Bill and I were sent to Harrisburg to do something. Fact is we could do nothing as the two caucuses were meeting to resolve the crisis. Upon returning, Bill informed the Chancellor we had led the way to the resolution. Bill was one of the funniest human beings I ever knew, along with his modesty In leadership.

I was working in Washington, D.C., for a year, living in a "garden" apartment in a house near DuPont Circle. Camille Bullock owned the house. In her mid-80s, Camille was devoted to the arts, to include antiques. She was well informed and educated in world and domestic affairs. Whenever she worked on the "garden" level we had wonderful conversations. Easy to recall and admire? Absolutely. But just in case, she gave us priceless gifts for our home.

How is one to describe Nelson W. Polsby? Not in a paragraph, that's for sure. A brilliant wit, Nelson commanded a room. He devoured data, categorized and stored them, and invited their use in discussion and debate, over which he typically towered. I liked being with him, especially in his back garden where we both sought to amuse the other. Nelson preceded me in managing the American Political Science Review. Pat Patterson followed us both. Quite a triple threat.

I met Robert A. Katzmann at The Brookings Institution in Washington, D. C. He directed the Governance Institute which sponsored programs on legislative, judicial, and executive agencies and programs. The institute was a Katzmann creation. He raised the money, he organized its operations. Bob was widely knowledgeable of all aspects of governance. Subsequently, he was appointed U. S. Circuit Judge for the Second Circuit, New York City. He served as Chief Judge for seven years. During our time at Brookings, Bob and I frequently dined together, followed by long walks. He was a gentle, modest, highly informed, and creative person, from whom I sought to emulate both in style and substance.

Proper management of an institution requires highly sensitive skills, prime of which is sensitivity to success of its membership. Tom Mann directed the governmental affairs division of The Brookings Institution. Tom measured his achievement by the success of those in the division. His style was in the smile. One could learn much about human relations by observing his leadership. Additionally, he was an accomplished scholar of Washington politics, often working with Norman Ornstein at the American Enterprise Institute. The two of them stimulated an enormous amount of scholarship of and participation in national politics. I was one of the beneficiaries.

In moving to the University of Wisconsin-Madison in 1988 I was able to observe the leadership of Chancellor Donna Shalala. I was returning to the university from which I received my graduate degrees. Donna was the first woman to lead as Chancellor. What a pleasure to watch her masterful style. Unsurprisingly, she was then appointed Secretary of Health and Human Services in the first Bill Clinton Administration—serving during his full eight years in office.

I first met Byron Shafer as a graduate student working with Nelson Polsby at Berkeley. He impressed me greatly, mature beyond his years, knowledgeable beyond his training. Later he was appointed to an endowed professorship at Oxford University, Nuffield College. In 1998-99 I observed him manage seminars at Nuffield. Wow! I came to realize how I should have been doing it all those years. But even more than that, I had a full year to benefit from my intellectual partnership with Byron. That companionship continued into my retirement.

One additional pair kept popping up as influential in this exercise. Reflecting on our two sons, Joseph and Daniel, has been flat out inspirational. Now 61 and 59 respectivelythey have shaped their lives so as to bring joy and pride to their parents. Their careers, Joe as an arecheologist, Dan as a writer and editor, have been immensely successful. Additionally and importantly, each has been a model father, Joe to Annabel, Dan to Phoebe and Nathaniel. Vera and I have been incredibly grateful to them, suggesting this piece of advice to you: Retire to a loving family.

These reminiscences are but a sample of those who help shape my academic career. It would be difficult to identify specific impacts of each person. But combined they offer a broad direction or theme to my goals and purposes. That justifies my urging readers to try re-imagining their careers, specifically seeking to identify who contributed what to their careers. Think forward along the way, perhaps how one piece fit with what and who came along next. I hope and trust you will find the exercise as enjoyable as I did.

<u>Well, You Have To.</u> I have come to the end of my display of CHUCK'S help for recent retirees. The dominant theme has been variability of the retirement experience. Above all, retirees should prepare themselves to cope with the physical, mental, personal, and neighboring changes defining your new life. Complicating this process is the uncertainty of what will happen, when and how changes will occur, and with what impact. CHUCK can only provide hints as help. At least, however, CHUCK has lived long enough to provide a time factor—25 years of retirement with his partner, Vera.

Mentioning Mrs. Jones raises vital matters for why "you have to ASK CHUCK." It is simple really. CHUCK'S retirement has moved along smoothly as a consequence of his partnership with Vera. ASK CHUCK who manages their banking? Answer: Vera. Ask him who arranges their social life? Vera. They eat healthfully—who produces that result? Right again, Vera. What about knitting baby sweaters for grandparent friends? Vera makes them all. Guess who cleans up after the dog throws up? Dear Vera.

Who drives their cars, bought the most recent one, and schedules the oil changes? Bingo—Vera. Who monitors their dog's vet appointments, not to mention CHUCK'S visits with various docs? Yes, you got it right again. Who do the grandkids call? Grandma Vera. Take note: CHUCK rarely uses the phone but is quite at ease with email. Oops, almost forgot, decades ago Vera taught him how to swim and ski! Ssssh... And who was CHUCK'S ski partner, moving gracefully down the slopes for so many years? Wow, was that ever fun! With whom did CHUCK waltz at the Wintergreen Austrian dinner? His Austrian born wife, Vera.

You can't have Vera, of course, devoted as she has been to CHUCK for 63 years of marriage. However, she understands the retirement gig and needed no help from him for how she might contribute to its effective play out. No training was required. In fact, their lives never worked that way. So whatever adjustments were required in the partnership happened naturally and cooperatively with each role self-defined.

So there it is. You have to—both of you if there are two. Retire purposely, gracefully, even joyfully together and all else will fall into place.

Printed in the United States
by Baker & Taylor Publisher Services